CW00322195

1 MONTH OF
FREE
READING

at
www.ForgottenBooks.com

By purchasing this book you are eligible for one month membership to ForgottenBooks.com, giving you unlimited access to our entire collection of over 1,000,000 titles via our web site and mobile apps.

To claim your free month visit: www.forgottenbooks.com/free523053

ISBN 978-0-484-38090-4
PIBN 10523053

This book is a reproduction of an important historical work. Forgotten Books uses
state-of-the-art technology to digitally reconstruct the work, preserving the original format
whilst repairing imperfections present in the aged copy. In rare cases, an imperfection in
the original, such as a blemish or missing page, may be replicated in our edition. We do,
however, repair the vast majority of imperfections successfully; any imperfections that
remain are intentionally left to preserve the state of such historical works.

For support please visit www.forgottenbooks.com

THE

CONSEQUENCES & AMELIORATIONS

OF

BLINDNESS.

(A BRIEF SKETCH).

BY

WILLIAM MOON, LL.D.,

AUTHOR OF "LIGHT FOR THE BLIND," ETC.

London:

LONGMANS & CO., PATERNOSTER ROW.

1875.

EDWARD VERRALL,
PRINTER,
BRIGHTON.

PREFACE.

It is surprising that so few persons are aware of the vast number of the Blind in the World, their peculiar condition and special requirements.

The following pages present a brief sketch of these subjects, together with an account of the various means which already exist, and of others yet required, for the alleviation of the physical, mental, and pecuniary distresses, consequent upon Blindness.

The author indulges the hope that many, from the perusal of this little work, may be led to assist, by their means and influence, in furthering the philanthropic and necessary schemes therein referred to.

W. MOON, LL.D.

104, Queen's Road, Brighton,
April, 1875.

CONTENTS.

BLINDNESS.

What is blindness? It is one of our greatest calamities. It shuts out from the eye the view of all material objects, and it is accompanied by a train of mental, physical, and pecuniary privations. ·

The effulgent rays of the golden sun, the soft pale light of the silvery moon, the bright twinkling of countless myriads of stars, the gorgeous tints on hill and vale, on tree and flower, and the smiling faces of loving relatives and friends, are all shut out from the blind. The most glowing and graphic description of the marvellous works of nature and art may excite the imagination of those who have become blind in early life, but must ever fail to convey to them more than a partial conception of the beauties of surrounding objects. All remains invisible. The darkened human dwelling-house is impenetrable to a single ray of light to gladden the eye and cheer the heart. As Milton plaintively exclaims, in reference to his own blindness :

> " Dark, dark, dark, amid the blaze of noon;
> Irrecoverably dark, total eclipse,
> Without all hope of day ! "

And in his " Invocation to Light," Milton makes the following touching allusion to his blindness :

" Thus with the year
Seasons return ; but not to me returns
Day, or the sweet approach of even or morn,
Or sight of vernal bloom, or summer's rose,
Or flocks, or herds, or human face divine ;
But cloud instead, and ever-during dark
Surrounds me: from the cheerful ways of men
Cut off, and for the book of knowledge fair
Presented with a universal blank
Of nature's works to me expunged and rased,
And wisdom at one entrance quite shut out.
So much the rather thou celestial Light
Shine inward, and the mind through all her powers
Irradiate.   There plant eyes, all mist from thence
Purge and disperse, that I may see and tell
Of things invisible to mortal sight."

Such, and much more than has been described, are the peculiar deprivations of the blind ; and whilst those who can see, must acknowledge the blessing of sight, a natural sympathy is evoked to relieve and succour those less-favoured than themselves.

Societies, Schools, and other Institutions, have been established, having for their aim the spiritual, intellectual, and industrial welfare of the blind ; placing within their reach the means of reading the Bible for themselves,— thus illuminating their minds with the cheering rays of divine truth,—as well as providing the means for their temporal comfort and support. By the aid of the numerous tangible contrivances which have been devised for their use, the sense of touch becomes the handmaid to the intellect; and thus, by means of Embossed Reading, Maps, and Diagrams, a blind person may gain, in some measure, a knowledge of surrounding objects, and even of the heavenly bodies, their magnitudes, motions, and influences.

A list of the Schools, Workshops, Home Teaching Societies, and Free Lending Libraries, &c., together with the addresses and nature of the Charities for the relief of those unable to earn their livelihood by any trade, will be found on pages 28, 29, &c.

NUMBER OF THE BLIND.

The Blind in the United Kingdom of Great Britain and Ireland number about 30,000. The aggregate number of the blind in the world cannot be less than 3,000,000.

There were in England and Wales, in 1871, according to the Census of that year, blind private gentlemen, 270; ladies, 665; clergymen, 21; nonconformist ministers, 14; musicians, 352; shoemakers, 131; army pensioners, 78; grocers and tea-dealers, 135; seamen, 134; farmers, 331; agricultural labourers, 495; miners, 275; labourers (undefined), 441; female domestic servants, 122; laundresses, 84.

It is remarkable that only 4 law clerks, 1 engraver, and 14 watch and clock makers, appear in the list.

NUMBER OF BLIND PERSONS IN ENGLAND AND WALES,

ALSO THE NUMBER IN THE LONDON DISTRICT,

Taken from the Census Returns for 1871.

Ages.	ENGLAND AND WALES.			LONDON DISTRICT.		
	Males.	Females.	Total.	Males.	Femls.	Total.
From 1 to 5	290	277	567	32	35	67
,, 5 ,, 10	397	303	700	44	39	83
,, 10 ,, 15	490	381	871	79	63	142
,, 15 ,, 20	489	392	881	69	62	131
,, 20 ,, 25	493	411	904	60	63	123
,, 25 ,, 30	467	357	824	62	64	126
,, 30 ,, 35	588	410	998	77	60	137
,, 35 ,, 40	657	387	1044	75	63	138
,, 40 ,, 45	744	411	1155	95	66	161
,, 45 ,, 50	707	452	1159	94	81	175
,, 50 ,, 55	839	596	1435	116	111	227
,, 55 ,, 60	799	644	1443	100	102	202
,, 60 ,, 65	865	840	1705	105	142	247
,, 65 ,, 70	893	893	1786	103	143	246
,, 70 ,, 75	927	1113	2040	79	189	268
,, 75 ,, 80	848	995	1843	80	113	193
,, 80 ,, 85	574	751	1325	43	88	131
,, 85 ,, 90	242	418	660	25	41	66
,, 90 ,, 95	57	150	207	6	15	21
,, 95 ,, 100	11	30	41	2	4	6
,, 100 & up.	1	1	2	0	0	0
Total...	11,378	10,212	21,590	1,346	1,544	2,890

SCOTLAND.

The total number of blind in Scotland, in 1871, was 3,019. Males, 1,490; females, 1,529. Under 5 years of age, 134; from 5 to 10, 103; from 10 to 15, 135; from 15 to 20, 143; from 20 to 30, 248; from 30 to 40, 281; from 40 to 50, 325; from 50 to 60, 380; from 60 to 70, 471; from 70 to 80, 533; from 80 to 90, 300; from 90 to 100, 51; from 100 upwards, 7.

IRELAND.

The total number of blind in Ireland, in 1861,* was 6,879. Under 15 years of age, 340; from 15 to 30, 1,116; from 30 to 50, 1,579; from 50 to 70, 2,310; from 70 to 80, 868; from 80 upwards, 654.

CAUSES OF BLINDNESS.

The causes of blindness vary considerably. Of late years, owing to the great advances of medical science, but few comparatively, in our own country, become blind previous to adolescence. The major portion become so after 30 years of age, and principally from the three following causes :—

(1) Accidents in hazardous callings.

(2) Inflammation of the eyes of various kinds, which are incidental to persons of all ages and stations.

(3) Over-work, or advancing years.

CONSEQUENCES OF BLINDNESS.

It is obvious that, as blindness closes the chief avenue

---

* The publication of the Irish Census Returns for 1871 is not yet completed.

for acquiring knowledge, and very frequently deprives the sufferer of the means of subsistence, dependance upon others must necessarily more or less ensue.

The Bible, or other books, which previously may have been sources of mental refreshment and recreation, become sealed to the sightless, unless they be read to them by others, or that they be provided with a tangible means of gaining their contents for themselves. It matters not whether the affliction alight upon the ploughman, the clerk, the merchant, the nobleman, or the king upon his throne, to each the same remark applies.

THE PECUNIARY LOSSES CONSEQUENT ON BLINDNESS.

Numerous are the instances in which blindness has plunged husbands and fathers, with their wives and families, into the deepest poverty and distress.

And who can fully estimate their melancholy condition?

Speaking of the blind of Glasgow, Mr. Barnhill, who has carefully investigated the condition of this class in that city, states that 148 men and 66 women, who had come under his notice, were attacked with blindness whilst following their occupations. Of the 148 men, 26 were still in comparatively favourable circumstances, although great losers by their blindness. The result with respect to the remaining 122, after making full allowance for their income as blind persons, shows an average loss of 18 shillings per week,—that is, £46 16s. per annum for each individual, or for the total number £5,709 12s. per annum. The result of a similar estimate for the 66 women, after making allowance for their present income, shows an average loss of 4 shillings per week, or £10 8s. per annum individually, or a total of about £686 8s. per annum. The combined loss of the 148 men and 66 women being nearly £6,400 per annum.

SCHOOLS AND WORKSHOPS FOR EMPLOYING THE BLIND.

At the Schools for the blind and the various Workshops which have been established in many of the principal towns of this country, to give instruction and employment to those deprived of sight, numerous trades are taught : such as basket, brush, mat, and matting making ; mattress and bed making ; carpet, rug, sack, rope, and twine making ; also shoe making, chair seating, and various kinds of bead, knitting, netting, sewing, and crochet work. Some of the blind are very skilful in playing the organ, in teaching music and singing, and in tuning pianofortes. Others are engaged in cutting firewood, and in selling various articles, such as tea, &c., &c. A large number of the blind, by means of the Workshops, procure employment, which enables many of them to contribute considerably to the support of themselves and their families. Great encouragement and assistance might be afforded to the Committees of the various Institutions in carrying out their benevolent efforts, if the public more generally purchased the articles manufactured by the blind, which are usually of good quality and at moderate prices. It would greatly benefit the blind, if the number of Workshops could be largely increased.

READING FOR THE BLIND.

One of the greatest alleviations of the deprivation of

sight, is the use of Embossed Reading, which was introduced at Paris about the year 1784, when the books were first embossed in Italic letters, and afterwards, in 1817, in the large and small Roman letters. These were followed, in Scotland, in 1827, by Gall's angular type, and, in 1837, by Alston's Roman type. From that time to the present, various modifications of the common letter have been introduced in Great Britain, Germany, and America. These have all been found too difficult for the majority of the blind to decipher, in consequence of the numerous lines and intricate forms of which many of the letters are composed.* The stenographic systems of Messrs. Frere and Lucas, although consisting of simple characters, are burdened with numerous contractions, difficult for the aged, the nervous, and the uneducated blind to acquire and retain. Braille's dotted system, in its original and modified forms, although useful to children, is also found unsuitable for the adult, if he be accustomed to rough manual labour, or advanced in years.

ORIGIN AND PECULIARITIES OF MOON'S SYSTEM OF EMBOSSED READING.

In the year 1840, when I became blind, I discovered,

---

* The Council of the British and Foreign Blind Association have expressed their opinion as follows :—" The Roman character in all its existing forms is so complicated, that it requires long education and great acuteness of touch to read it with ease ; and its universal adoption would be tantamount to the total exclusion of the great majority of the blind from the privilege of reading."

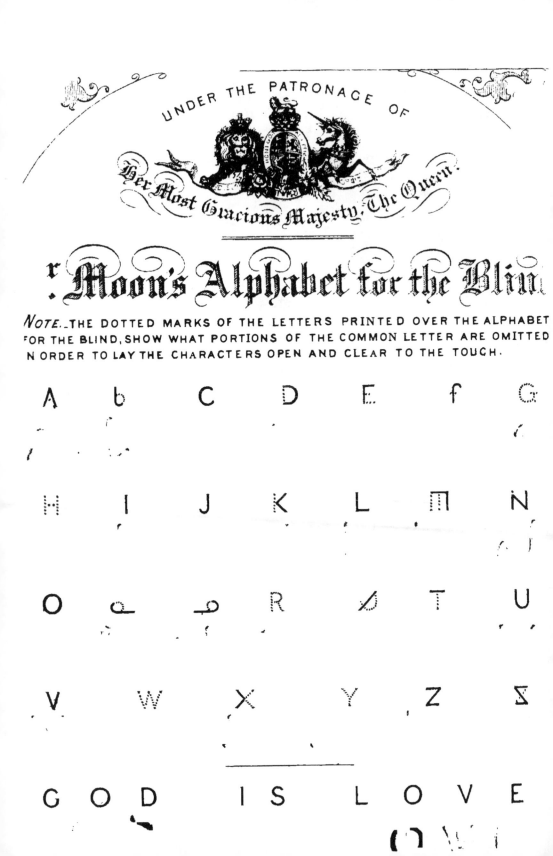

UNDER THE PATRONAGE OF

Her Most Gracious Majesty, The Queen.

ᵣ Moon's Alphabet for the Blind

NOTE.—THE DOTTED MARKS OF THE LETTERS PRINTED OVER THE ALPHABET FOR THE BLIND, SHOW WHAT PORTIONS OF THE COMMON LETTER ARE OMITTED N ORDER TO LAY THE CHARACTERS OPEN AND CLEAR TO THE TOUCH.

A b C D E f G

H I J K L ⊓ N

O ᵓ ᵔ R ∕ T U

V W X Y Z ∑

G O D   I S   L O V E

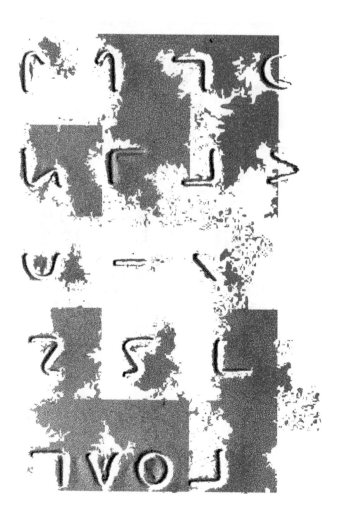

with much regret, that the arduous efforts of my good and zealous predecessors had failed to accomplish the object to which they had been directed. From various circumstances I was led to investigate the causes of failure, and to attempt the construction of a System of Reading adapted to all classes and ages of the blind. By the Divine blessing upon my endeavours, I was enabled to project a plan embracing very Simple Characters for the Alphabet, which is composed principally of the Roman Letters in their original or slightly-modified forms, combined with *Full Orthography*. Some few of the more complex letters of the Roman Alphabet could not be altered to advantage, and I therefore substituted new characters in their stead ; and when the Alphabet was completed, it was found to consist of only *Nine* Characters of very simple formation placed in various positions.

The Alphabet is of universal application, and has been adapted to 80 different languages, comprising the principal European and Asiatic languages, as well as several of the African and North American.

Since the commencement of embossing the Bible and other books upon my plan, in 1847, until 1875, nearly 100,000 volumes have been circulated !

MOON'S LIBRARY FOR THE BLIND.

The Library in Moon's Type for the Blind now comprises, in addition to the Holy Scriptures and a large number of Single Chapters, 37 volumes of Religious Works, 53 Biographies, 49 volumes of Tales and Anecdotes, 27 of Poetry, 4 of History of England, 2 of Geography, 4 of Biblical Dictionary, 1 of Natural History, 1 of Astronomy, an Atlas of the Stars, a Primer, several Easy Reading Books, a Spelling Book, a Grammar, and many volumes in Foreign languages.

SUCCESS OF MOON'S READING AMONG THE BLIND.

The success attending this improved system, may be briefly summarised as follows.

Many, who for years had made futile attempts to learn by other systems, have easily accomplished *this;* and many of those who could read before losing their sight, have learnt it in one lesson.

Many men and women working at such trades as basket, rug, rope, and mat making, by which their fingers become hardened, and consequently their sense of touch diminished, after fruitlessly endeavouring to learn by other plans, have acquired this with remarkable facility, and were soon able to read with ease and rapidity.

Persons advanced in years, and those whose nerves have been shaken by accident, or impaired by disease, have easily learnt the system ; and the Reading has, in numerous instances, become to them an inexpressible solace and pleasure.

Scarcely anything more melancholy can be imagined than such a threefold affliction as being blind, deaf, and dumb ! Nevertheless, many thus afflicted have learnt to read, and delight in the use of the books.

Ministers of various denominations are occasionally, by blindness, cut off from pursuing their public duties ;

but by means of these books, several have been enabled to resume them.

The numbers of Readers by this system it would be difficult fully to compute; but it may with certainty be said, that there are many thousands of blind in the United Kingdom and in foreign countries enjoying the inestimable privileges the system bestows. Amongst the Readers may be found persons of many classes and conditions. The peer and the peasant, the young and the old, the learned and the illiterate; the divine, the physician, the surgeon, the artizan, the labourer, the soldier and sailor, all alike, have partaken of the blessing which the Reading affords.*

---

* Mr. Buckle, the Superintendent of the Yorkshire School for the Blind, writes in the Report of that Institution for 1874 as follows:—"It is now pretty generally admitted that the type invented by Dr. Moon is much easier than any form of Roman type. The adult blind, as a rule, prefer it; so do our own pupils. Boys whose hands are hardened by basket-work can feel it, when they are quite at a loss with the Roman. And seeing that, in various parts of Yorkshire, Libraries for the blind have been founded, consisting of books in this type, mainly at the expense of Sir Charles Lowther, Bart., of Wilton Castle, Redcar, Yorkshire, it is quite evident that we must teach it at York."

To the various Home-Teaching Societies and Free Lending Libraries in Yorkshire, Sir C. H. Lowther has, altogether, kindly presented 3,294 volumes. To these might be added 5,047 volumes which he has so munificently given to Libraries, &c., in other parts of our country, and 1,568 volumes to America, Australia, &c., making the large total of 9,909 volumes in the

B

Wherever the system has been tried, whether in France, Germany, Holland, Italy, Spain, Denmark, Norway, Sweden, Turkey, Syria, Egypt, India, China, America, or in our Colonies, it has proved equally acceptable and successful.

SOCIETIES FOR TEACHING THE BLIND TO READ AT THEIR OWN HOMES,

AND FOR SUPPLYING THEM WITH BOOKS ON MOON'S SYSTEM FROM FREE LENDING LIBRARIES.

These Societies have been established in many of the principal cities and towns of our own and other countries.

The London Society, one of the first established, now employs 11 teachers, who search out and teach the blind to read at their own homes, in London and its neighbourhood. The Report for the year ending March, 1874, states that, during that period, 23,712 visits had been made; 28,629 volumes had been circulated in connection with the Free Lending Libraries; and 1,419 pupils were upon the Register, 819 of whom were able to read!

In addition to what has been accomplished in London and its neighbourhood, the Society is exerting itself in the promotion of the Home-Teaching scheme in various parts of England. The Edinburgh and Glasgow Societies are doing similar work in Scotland. By means of such organizations a large amount of good has been

---

short space of five years. Were this benevolent example followed in every county of Great Britain, the blind poor, throughout the length and breadth of our ~~own and other~~ land, might soon have Free Libraries within their reach.

effected at a comparatively small expense; and it is hoped that by means of such agencies all the blind of the United Kingdom may soon be afforded the opportunity of learning to read. The benefit of Free Lending Libraries to the blind must be self-evident, and is a boon which may be conferred, at a comparatively small expense, upon the blind of any neighbourhood, if a few friends will subscribe together to promote such an object. Not less than 100,000 volumes are being circulated annually amongst the blind poor from the Free Lending Libraries now formed.

For further particulars upon the subject of "Home-Teaching," *vide* "*Light for the Blind*" and the Reports of the several Home-Teaching Societies. The Secretary of the London Society, 34, New Bridge Street, Blackfriars, will gladly afford information respecting the Home-Teaching Movement.

EDUCATION OF THE BLIND IN ORDINARY SCHOOLS.

Experience for many years, in this and other countries, has proved that, with but little effort on the part of Teachers, blind children can easily be educated in Ordinary Schools. A number of the sighted children can quickly be taught my embossed alphabet (as it always has the common alphabet printed over it in black letters); and when they have learnt, the blind child or children may readily be taught by them to read. This will avoid occupying the Master's time, and prevent his being taken from the other duties of his School. If two or three lessons were given upon the black board by the Master, the whole School would soon learn my embossed reading, as the sighted pupils might copy the characters upon their slates, and would thus become more familiar with them. If this method were adopted in all our Schools, thousands of children might soon be fitted to instruct the Blind, not only in the Schools, but at their own homes, and thus a kindly and sympathising feeling would be created towards those who are blind. It has been remarked by Inspectors of Schools and others, that blind children thus educated, very frequently profit more from the oral instruction than the sighted ones, and that those who assist the Teacher in the instruction of the blind children, advance more rapidly than the rest of the scholars. The London School Board, after full enquiry into the subject, have resolved to adopt my system of Reading, and have secured the co-operation of the London Home-Teaching Society in teaching the blind children admitted into their Schools ;* thus avoiding any difficulty or hindrance that might be anticipated on the part of the Masters or Mistresses. The Home-Teacher, in engaging the assistance of one or more of the sighted scholars explains to them how they may help the blind, and thus the instruction is carried on during the interval of the Teacher's visits. There will doubtless be but few instances where the School Teachers will not take sufficient interest in directing the teaching of the Blind themselves.

Children thus primarily educated, are the better prepared for subsequent admission into Schools for the

---

* The London School Board have decided to appoint a *special teacher* of the blind in their Schools.

Blind, which possess special advantages and facilities for the teaching and practice of Music, Trades, &c.

The instruction of Blind children in Ordinary Schools is by no means a new idea. For many years I have advocated its adoption; and we have, at different times, sent a large number of books from Brighton to various places both at home and abroad, for the education of blind children in Schools for the sighted; and very pleasing testimonies have been received from China, India, Egypt,* Syria, Australia, Turkey, and other countries, in reference to the results of teaching children in Mission and other Schools. Many children have also been taught in Sunday Schools.

The Report of the Edinburgh Asylum for the Blind (1874), states that 40 years ago the Directors sent a number of Blind Boys to the Sessional School, where, under the tuition of Mr. Wood, they made admirable and satisfactory progress.

The Report for 1874, of the Glasgow Home-Teaching Society for the Blind, gives a very interesting account of the efforts of the Committee and their active superintendent, Mr. Barnhill, during the past six years, in promoting the education of Blind children in Ordinary Schools.

Similar efforts of other Home-Teaching Societies have been equally successful.

It is very advisable that children should be taught a system of Embossed Reading which, in future years, they

---

* I am informed that a large number of the Schoolmasters of Egypt are blind, and that they rank amongst the most literary men of the country.

will retain the faculty of deciphering; thus avoiding the necessity of acquiring a second method together with a new set of books.

From time to time, additional *Educational Books*, suitable for the blind in Ordinary Schools, will be embossed in my type.

HOW *TWENTY* GIRLS POSSESSED OF SIGHT LEARNT MOON'S EMBOSSED TYPE IN

LESS THAN ONE HOUR,

WITH THE OBJECT OF *TEACHING* THEIR *BLIND SCHOOL-FELLOWS* AND NEIGHBOURS TO READ.

The following extract of a letter from the late much-lamented Mrs. Bowen Thompson, of Beirut, sufficiently illustrates the ease with which blind children may, in *ordinary Schools*, be taught to read, even though it be in a distant land and in a foreign tongue, and the sympathy and interest at once evoked by the sighted scholars in assisting their blind companions to read for themselves, without incurring but little extra labour on the part of the Master or Mistress.

Writing from Beirut, Mrs. Thompson says : "We had a charming day with our dear children on Sunday afternoon. Moon's system for teaching the blind to read excited great interest among our dear girls. Seated in their midst, under the shade of the Zeuzaleh Avenue, and inhaling the sea-breezes from the deep-blue Mediterranean, I took Moon's Gospel of St. John, with the sight of which many had become familiar from seeing little blind Jasmine, the Druse girl, learning to read it in the Elementary School. I commenced with teaching the Alphabet to six of the elder pupils; but it was delightful to see the younger ones flocking round,—some seated on the door-steps, some standing behind, and others sitting on the pebbled pavement. As each girl was asked her letters, the others would beg, 'May I say it, I know it?' and then, instead of six children, *some twenty learnt to read their Alphabet in less than an hour!* They then commenced writing words on their slates, and succeeded so well, that I left them to write out the first verse of the 1st Chapter of St. John. On my returning, an hour afterwards, I found that Feridi and Hannie had both written out some six verses in the Characters.

" I then told the children of the conversation to which it was once my privilege to listen, which took place at the Barnet Conference, between Dr. Moon and some fifteen blind persons, who were seated in a circle in Mr. Pennefather's beautiful Parsonage grounds. They became more and more concerned for the blind; and when I asked who would teach the blind during the holidays, many hands were lifted up; when some dear children looked very sorrowful, and said, 'But I don't know any blind whom I can teach!'

" By way of encouragement, I told those of the girls who I felt could really teach, that I would write to the Bible Society in England, and ask them to give an English Reference Bible, with gilt edges, to any girl whom I could report as having taught a blind person to read the Bible. Bright and full of hope, they exclaimed, 'I hope the Bible Society will have to send many beautiful Bibles; all the girls will teach a blind child to read!' Hannie said, 'I hope I shall have three blind pupils, for there are three blind children near our house.' Dear little Miriam F., who lives in a grand house standing by itself, seemed perplexed how she could get to any blind person. Suddenly her countenance brightened up, and she said, 'There is a poor blind man living near our house; I will teach him!' Some of the girls said, 'Would it not be a shame for Miriam to teach an old man?' I said, 'Not at all; God will bless the efforts of little Miriam, as He did those of the little English girl who learnt to read the Irish Bible, that she might teach old Cornach to read the blessed book for himself.' I promised to procure ten copies of the Embossed Gospel of St. John.

"A more willing band of young Teachers for the blind, it will not be easy to procure."

HINTS TO TEACHERS OF ORDINARY SCHOOLS WITH REFERENCE TO THE INSTRUCTION OF BLIND CHILDREN.

I would suggest that the Master should give a lesson upon the black board to the entire School, first respecting the eight unaltered letters of the alphabet, then the fourteen altered ones, and lastly the five new characters; the children at the same time writing the letters upon their slates. Care should be taken to describe what portions of the ordinary letters are omitted, to make the embossed characters open and clear to the touch of the Blind. If the Teacher has not sufficient time to devote to the instruction of the children from the black board, it will be sufficient to explain the system from one of the embossed alphabets. When the children appear to understand the alphabet, two lines of reading should be given upon the black board,—the first line from left to right, the second from right to left,—to show that the Blind read in this way, to prevent their losing the line, or time, in reading. The commencement of the Lord's Prayer would form a good reading lesson, as the children would more readily comprehend it, the prayer being familiar to them. A copy of the Embossed Alphabet and Lord's Prayer, if hung up in the Schoolroom, would form an attraction, and might induce many to take an interest in the Reading for the Blind. Printed Instructions accompany every copy of the embossed alphabet.

SUGGESTIONS TO PARENTS OF BLIND CHILDREN.

Sighted children acquire their habits, to a great extent, by imitation. A child deprived of sight, however, must be EDUCATED in all its habits. It should early be trained to a self-dependance. It should be encouraged, as early as sighted children, to wash, dress, and feed itself; to comb and brush its own hair, to lace its boots, &c. Every effort should be made to correct irregular habits in walking, sitting, and standing. The earlier a child is taught to read, the better, as it affords occupation both for the mind and the fingers.

PREPARATORY SCHOOLS FOR BLIND CHILDREN.

Special Preparatory Institutions are required for children

of 5 or 6 years of age ; although, as I have already re-marked, much may be done in the education of blind children in our Ordinary Schools. An early preparatory education, and training to wash, dress, and in other ways assist themselves, would tend greatly to facilitate subsequent efforts to fit the Blind for mixing in society and obtaining a livelihood, which they now often fail to do from the want of having received this initiatory tuition.

HIGHER EDUCATION FOR THE BLIND.

The remarks which have been already made respecting the education of the blind poor in Ordinary Schools, are equally applicable to children of the wealthy. There is scarcely a limit to the proficiency to which they may attain. The highest academical honours, and even university professorships, are not beyond their acquisition.

At various times and places Private and Public Colleges and Schools have been opened for imparting a superior education to the blind. Mr. Foster's College at the Commandery, Worcester, for the education of the blind sons of gentlemen, may be considered as the representative of the former ; and of the latter, the Royal Normal College at Norwood has hitherto proved the most successful.

Here the inmates number about 50, who receive a good sound general education ; but the principal aim of the Council is, to have imparted to those who possess the ability, a thorough knowledge of music and the use of various musical instruments, thereby enabling them to become efficient musicians and tuners. A visit to the College will afford interesting proof of what can be accomplished in this department of education.

OUTLINE MAP

OF THE

BRITISH ISLES,

BY

W. MOON, LL.D., F.R.G.S.

SHETLANDS

Mainland

ORKNEYS

C.Wrath   Mainland

Murray Firth   Kinnard Hd

ATLANTIC OCEAN

SCOTLAND

NORTH SEA

HEBRIDES

SKYE

INVERNESS   ABERDEEN

Mull

Firth of Forth

Islay

GLASGOW   EDINBURGH   BERWICK

BELFAST

Donegal Bay   Solway Firth   ENGLAND   YORK   Flamborough Hd

I OF MAN

DUBLIN   LIVERPOOL   The Wash

GALWAY   R.Liffey   ANGLESEA

Galway B.   BIRMINGHAM   NORWICH

R.Shannon   IRELAND   WEXFORD   WALES

CORK   BRISTOL   LONDON   R.Thames

IRISH CHANNEL   R.Severn   DOVER   Strait of D

Lundy I.   BRIGHTON

C.Clear   PLYMOUTH   WIGHT   CALAIS

I OF

LANDSEND   ENGLISH CHANNEL

Scilly Is   ALDERNEY   DIEPPE

Lizard   GUERNSEY   HAVRE   FRANCE

JERSEY

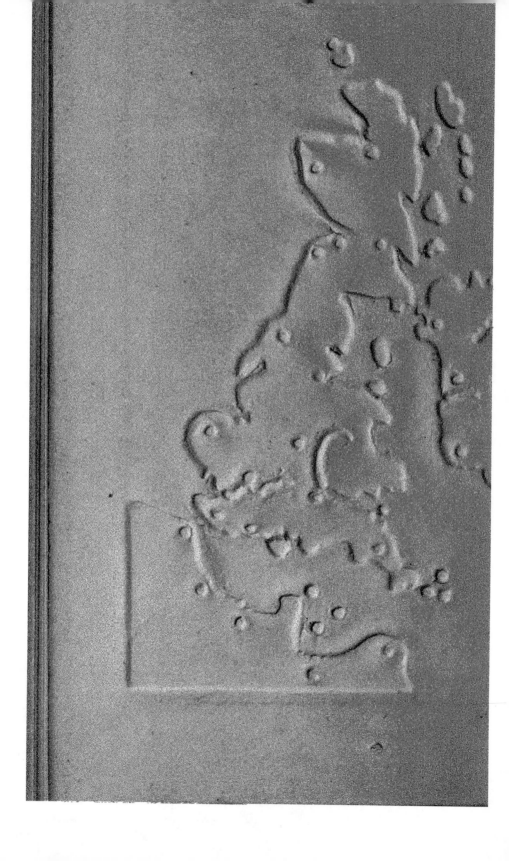

The employment of models in the instruction of the Blind might be more generally adopted in this country, as I have known them to be of great use in several of the continental Schools.

MUSICAL INSTRUCTION FOR THE BLIND.

The Blind may be taught to play a variety of instruments, but it is well to confine pupils to one, or at most two, until they become proficient. If they are to excel in music, their tuition should commence early, and the instruction and practice should be frequent and regular. If a blind child is to be prepared for a musical career, it is essential that he should, up to the age of 14 years, devote his time entirely to the study of music and other branches of a general education ; as, before that age, it would be of little advantage to put him to any special kind of handicraft.

HOW TO SECURE AN EFFICIENT AND IN-EXPENSIVE STAFF OF TEACHERS IN SCHOOLS FOR THE BLIND.

It has frequently been remarked by the Masters and Mistresses of Schools for the Blind that the progress of their pupils is retarded for the want of a larger staff of Teachers. Usually the teaching chiefly devolves upon the Master or Mistress ; but I would suggest that the more advanced pupils should give lessons in the various branches of instruction to those less advanced. This would greatly assist the Master or Mistress, and at the same time be a means of affording to the pupils the practice of teaching, and thus the better qualify them as Instructors when they leave school. In a school of 50 children there would probably not be less than 10 pupils sufficiently advanced to be capable, in some degree, of instructing others; and in teaching others, they themselves would be taught; and thus a large and efficient Staff of Teachers might soon be raised in a School, without much increase of expense to the funds of the Institution; but to effect this, and to stimulate the energies of the pupil-teachers or monitors, a small gratuity might be awarded them at stated periods, either quarterly, half-yearly, or yearly.

THE FUTURE OF BLIND SCHOLARS.

After every pains has been bestowed in the education of blind children, and large sums expended in the various Institutions for that purpose, the question yet remains, How are they to be directed into paths of self-supporting competency? On leaving School, they may possess the ability to play and teach the organ or some other musical instrument, tune pianofortes, make boots, mats, baskets, &c.; but they may still need the guiding hand and watchful care of the Committee and Friends of the School from whence they emanate, to enable them to establish themselves in their calling in some suitable neighbourhood, and it may be to provide them with the necessary means to do so by way of loan or gift, and otherwise interesting themselves among their friends and neighbours in getting them work by recommending them, occasionally calling on them at their homes, to see how they are progressing, and to encourage them by suitable counsels, &c. Those who follow the profession of music might be furnished with a Certificate of Merit, or other qualifications of proficiency.

SCHOOLS FOR THE BLIND IN THE UNITED KINGDOM.

ENGLAND.

London.—St. George's in the Fields, Southwark.—Avenue Road, Regent's Park.—The Alexandra Institution, Queen's Square.—Euston Road Institution.—Peckham.

Provinces.—Bath, Birmingham, Bolton, Brighton, Bristol, Exeter, Hastings, Liverpool, Leeds, Manchester, Newcastle, Norwich, Norwood, Nottingham, Plymouth, Preston, Southsea, Stockport, Worcester, York.

SCOTLAND.

Aberdeen, Dundee, Edinburgh, Glasgow.

IRELAND.

Dublin.—Molyneux.—Richmond.—Marlborough Street. —St. Mary's Catholic Asylum for Females, and one for Males.

Belfast, Cork, Limerick, Armagh.

FREE LENDING LIBRARIES AND HOME-TEACHING SOCIETIES FOR THE BLIND

Have been established at the following places. Those having Workshops in connection with them are marked thus *

ENGLAND.

London.—34, New Bridge Street, Blackfriars.—Peckham.

Provinces.—Alston, Barnsley, Bath, * Birmingham, * Bradford, Brighton, Bristol, * Carlisle, * Cheltenham, Cornwall (Redruth, &c.), Croydon, Derby, Dewsbury, Doncaster, Durham, Halifax, Huddersfield, * Hull, Ipswich, Isle of Wight, * Leeds, * Leicester, * Liverpool, Manchester, * Middlesborough, Newcastle-on-Tyne and Gateshead, Newport (Mon.), North Devon, Richmond, Rotherham, Scarborough, * Sheffield, Shrewsbury, Southampton, * Southsea, Staffordshire, Sunderland, Trowbridge, Wakefield, Whitby, Wolverhampton, * Worcester.

SCOTLAND.

* Aberdeen, Dundee, Edinburgh, Glasgow, Greenock, Inverness, Montrose, Orkney and Shetland, Paisley, Perth.

IRELAND.

Cork, * Dublin.

WALES.

* Cardiff, Newport, Swansea.

CHARITIES FOR GRANTING ANNUITIES, &c., TO THE BLIND.

Christian Blind Relief Society, 59, Burdett Road, Bow, London, E.   The relief afforded is 2s. 6d., 5s., or 10s. per month.

The Rev. W. Hethrington's Charity, Christ's Hospital, London.   Relief £10 per annum for persons over 61 years of age.

The Painters' Charity, Painters' Hall, Queenhithe, London. Relief £10 per annum for persons over 61 years of age.

The Blind Man's Friend, 29, Saville Row, London, gives from £12 to £20 per annum.

The Blind School, Southwark, grants annuities for 3 years.

Cames's Charity for the Blind, Cordwainers' Company, 43, Cannon Street West, London. Relief £5 per annum for men of not less than 46 years of age, and women of not less than 40 years of age.

Indigent Blind Relief Society, Red Lion Square, High Holborn, London.

Grainger's Pensions of £10 to the Blind. Trustees' address, Drapers' Hall, London.

Jews' Blind Relief Fund (for Jews only), 37, Duke Street, Aldgate, London.

The following are in connection with the *Clothworkers' Hall*, 41, Mincing Lane, London, E.C.

West's Charity. £5 per annum; age, 50 years and upwards.

Newman's Charity. £10 per annum; age, 50 years and upwards.

Thwaytes's Charity. £10 per annum; age, 50 years and upwards.

Hannah Acton's Charity. £10 per annum; age, 50 years and upwards.

Gregory's Charity. £4 per annum; age, 50 years and upwards.

Cornell's Charity. £10 per annum ; age, 50 years and upwards.

Love's Charity. £10 per annum ; age, 50 years and upwards.

———

The following are in connection with the *Goldsmiths' Hall*, Foster Lane, London, E.C.

Goldsmiths' Company Charity. £4 per annum.

Rachel Farmer's Charity. £4 per annum.

Cureton's Charity. £20 per annum.

Protestant Blind Relief Society, 12, Wellington Street, London Bridge, London, E.C. £3 per annum.

Humston's Vestry Hall Charity, St. Botolph's, Aldgate, London. £6 per annum ; for parishioners of St. Botolph's and S. Paul's, Shadwell.

Miss Horley's Charity, Messrs. Harrison & Beale, 19, Bedford Row, London, W.C. £20 per annum ; must be communicants of the Church of England.

———

Application should be made to the Secretaries of the various Institutions and Charities for further information respecting their objects, the conditions of admission, forms of application, &c. Scarcely any of these Charities afford assistance to persons who have, at any time, received parochial relief.

SUNDAY CLASSES FOR THE BLIND.

During the past 11 years I have held a Meeting of the Adult Blind, of Brighton, on Sunday afternoons, for

Specimens of
Dr. Moon's Type for the Blind.

AS APPLIED TO FOREIGN LANGUAGES.

English.

OU\ ΓΛ—•Γ\ Π•IC• Λ\— IN •ΓΛVΓN

French.

N O—\Γ ⊂Γ\Γ →UI Γ/ ΛU> CIΓU

German.

UΛ/Γ\ VΛ—Γ\ IN ⊃Π •IΠΓL.

Dutch.

OΝƆΓ VΛƆΓ\ .ƆIΓ IN ƆΓ •ΓΠΓLΓN

Danish.

VO\ VΛƆΓ\ .ƆU /OΠ I •IΠLΓNΓ.

Swedish.

ΓΛƆΓ\ VΛ\\ ./OΠ :Λ/— I •IΠLOΠ.

Russian.

OΠUL ⁼ΛΠ⊂ .C/Π IΛ ⁼Λ ⁼LLLCΛ

Arabic.

I—IUI IJΓ→ Ν→ IJΛΓOI/ J→/ZΠ .Λ IΛΓ

Armenian.

Π⊂ <—JΓ V/Γ ΠΓ /ΓΛIN:>Ν /U.

Greek.

the purpose of reading to them the Bible and other religious works, interspersed with prayer and addresses. The Meeting concludes with a tea, which is not unfrequently the first meal that some have partaken of during the day. These gatherings, I have good reason to believe, have been greatly blessed to many who have attended them, and have afforded opportunities for mutual intercourse and conversation,—a pleasure which is greatly appreciated.

I have also established a *Relief Fund* for those who attend these meetings ; and thus, for several winters, I have been enabled by subscriptions and gifts of Provisions, Coal, Clothing, &c., to supply them with Tea, Sugar, Bread, Meat, Potatoes, Coal, and Flannel and various other articles of wearing apparel. Without this aid some homes at " Happy Christmas-time," and during the subsequent months, would frequently have been uncheered and uncomforted either by firing, food, or necessary clothing.

TOWN, COUNTY, OR DISTRICT RELIEF FUND, FOR THE BLIND POOR.

As the plan of Relief last referred to has proved most successful in its operations, some similar well-devised efforts seem to suggest themselves for other large towns and districts.

Associations might be organised for counties, one of the principal towns being selected for head quarters. By a little effort on the part of the inhabitants of any locality, enough might be collected to make the condition of the blind poor more comfortable than it is at present. The relief afforded by the Charities previously referred to on pp. 30-1-2, has been something incalculable ; but additional aids are required for the succour of many thousands of the aged and distressed blind, which the existing Charities were not formed to relieve,—one condition for the eligibility of aid from such Charities being, in almost every instance, that the applicant shall not at any time have received parochial relief.

Some of the objects of such an organization as the one suggested might be :—

(1) To provide sums of money, as occasion may require, for those who have no source of income whatever, but are entirely dependant upon their relations and friends for support.

(2) To assist, by occasional supplementary aid, such as may be receiving a certain amount of relief from any of the special Charities or the Parochial Boards.

(3) To aid some by placing them in business, and to advance small sums of money for the purchase of materials to others who might have orders to execute which they could not otherwise undertake to do.

As the Blind are in the proportion of only 1 to the 1,000 of the general population, but little difficulty should be experienced in raising a fund in every county for the support of its own blind. Were every person to contribute but sixpence a-year, or one halfpenny per month, as a thank-offering for the blessing of sight, an income of £25 per annum would be provided for every blind person in our country.

ALMS-HOUSES FOR THE BLIND.

Alms-Houses would be a great boon to the blind, could they be provided in towns and districts where needed. The practicability of such a scheme is proved by the success of the Quinze-Vingts in Paris, where provision is made for 300 single and married blind persons.

GENERAL REMARKS AND HINTS TO THOSE DESIROUS OF HELPING THE BLIND.

Let all those who have it in their power, seek for blind persons in the surrounding district of their own residence, or of any place in which they may be temporarily located ; and if any be found who cannot read, supply them with an Embossed Alphabet, a Lord's Prayer, and a Single Chapter (the 14th of St. John, for instance), and then proceed to teach them according to the instructions given with each copy of the Alphabet.

A gentleman who endeavours to interest, on behalf of the Blind, all with whom he comes in contact, informs me that, during the past year, he has instructed not less than 50 sighted persons to read my embossed type,—each in the course of a quarter of an hour ; and he considers that, by the aid of the Alphabet and the accompanying Instructions, they were fitted to teach any blind persons with whom they might meet.

Those who have been taught to read, will feel grateful for a present of embossed books not in their possession. [See *List of Books*.]

There are some of the blind, however, who, from various causes, are incapable of learning to read by *any* system; and these claim even a larger sympathy from their more highly-favoured sighted friends and visitors. This sympathy may be shown by reading to them, by conversing with them, and by praying with them. Lastly, many of them are dependant upon poor parents, relatives, friends, and neighbours; and therefore, in addition to the kind offices of mental and spiritual aid, a little substantial assistance now and then would greatly help to smooth their rugged path of life.

WILLIAM MOON, LL.D.

104, Queen's Road, Brighton,
    Sussex, England.

APPENDIX.

BIOGRAPHICAL NOTES OF EMINENT BLIND PERSONS.

By way of encouragement, I have selected a few examples from the many instances on record of the extraordinary genius and ability displayed by the blind; showing that, although loss of sight is undoubtedly one of the greatest of deprivations, they have distinguished themselves in Literature, Divinity, Law, Physic, Mathematics, Astronomy, Music, and various other branches of Science and Art.

HOMER, "the Father of Song," completed his immortal "*Iliad*," and wrote "*The Odyssey*," after he had lost his eyesight.

MILTON wrote "*Paradise Lost*," "*Paradise Regained*," and "*Samson Agonistes*," when he was totally blind.

BLIND HARRY, the celebrated Scotch Minstrel, who was born blind, has been styled, from the excellence of his poetical compositions, "The Northern Homer."

NICHOLAS SAUNDERSON, LL.D., F.R.S., became blind in infancy. By his marvellous talents and perseverance, he became in his 29th year Lucasian Professor of Mathematics in the University of Cambridge, and was subsequently admitted a Fellow of the Royal Society.

NICAISE DE WERDE lost his sight at the age of three years. He became Professor of Common and Civil Law at the University of Cologne; and the degree of Doctor of Divinity was conferred upon him by the celebrated University of Louvaine.

THE REV. JOHN TROUGHTON, an eminent Puritan Divine, became blind at the age of four years. He received his rudimentary education at the Coventry Free School, and completed his studies at the University of Oxford, when he took the degree of Bachelor of Arts. He is the writer of several theological works of note.

DR. NICHOLAS BACON was deprived of sight at nine years of age. He studied at the University of Brussels, gained distinction among his fellow students, took his degree of Bachelor of Laws, and became an able Advocate in the Council of Brabant.

SIR JOHN FIELDING, the eminent Lawyer and Philanthropist, was blind from childhood, but was trained for the legal profession. On obtaining the necessary qualifications, he became a member of the Home Circuit; and on the failure of the health of his half-brother, Henry Fielding, he was appointed to succeed him as magistrate at Bow Street Police Court. Sir John Fielding's acuteness on the magisterial bench was remarkable. Whenever a crime of more than ordinary atrocity was committed in the Metropolis, "Blind Fielding, the thief-catcher," as he was called, was consulted by his brother justices, and his sagacity was seldom at fault. In his carriage, Sir John had a speaking pipe, by which he communicated with his coachman ; and when an obstruction occurred in the streets, he would ascertain from the coachman the nature of the impediment, and would call out of the carriage window, in an authoritative voice, to the driver of any particular vehicle to " move on," which caused no little surprise to the bystanders, and was the occasion of some enjoyment to the author of the joke. He was the founder of the Female Orphan Asylum, Lambeth, and took an active part in promoting the Marine Society and the Magdalen Hospital.

ZISCA, the Bohemian General and Reformer, was blind of one eye from childhood. At the siege of Rubi, in 1421, he was struck in the remaining eye by an arrow, from which he became totally blind. He nevertheless continued to hold the command. In all the battles and engagements he fought, he was but once defeated. Six times, in three campaigns, he vanquished the Emperor Sigismond in the open field, ravaged his towns, and laid waste his provinces ; thus reducing him to the greatest extremities, and compelling him to treat for peace upon equal terms.

JOHN STANLEY, D.M., an eminent English Musician, lost his sight when two years of age. His taste for music so rapidly developed, that, at the age of 11, he was appointed organist of All Hallows, Bread Street, London. Two years later, he was chosen, from a large number of candidates, organist of St. Andrew's, Holborn ; and eight years afterwards, the Benchers of the Honourable Society of the Inner Temple selected him as one of their organists. He was subsequently appointed Master of the King's Band; and his compositions evince great taste and judgment. It is said that "his abilities as an organist were so great, that it was no uncommon thing to see at the Temple, and at St. Andrew's, 30 or 40 organists waiting at the close of the service to hear the voluntary; and of this number, Handel often was one. Stanley's skill as a Musician was such that, when at a performance of one of Handel's "*Te Deums*," on finding the organ a semitone higher than the other instruments, he, without any premeditation, transposed the whole piece from D, into the key of seven sharps major; and it is doubtful whether there was, at that time, another performer in the Kingdom who would have attempted such a task.

GIOVANI GONNELLI is supposed to be the name of the Sculptor who executed a life-like bust of the Duke of Bracciano, in a cellar, where he was caused to perform his work, as the Duke doubted that he was blind. He also successfully sculptured a statue of Charles I. of England, and one of Pope Urban VIII., and obtained the patronage of the Duke of Tuscany and other illustrious personages.

M. BARET, JOSEPH KLEINHAUS, and others, deprived of sight, have likewise distinguished themselves as Sculptors and Carvers.

LIEUTENANT HOLMAN, R.N., one of the greatest blind Travellers, lost his sight on the West Coast of Africa, at the age of 25. Eight years afterwards he set forth alone upon a continental tour, and travelled through France, Italy, Savoy, Switzerland, Germany, and Holland. Shortly afterwards he attempted to traverse the whole extent of the Russian Empire; and had travelled a considerable distance into the interior, when he was arrested upon the charge of being a spy, and was brought back to the Austrian frontier. He then returned through Austria, Saxony, Prussia, and Hanover, to his native country. Subsequently he made a voyage round the World, in five years. He has related, in several volumes, the incidents of his travels.

JOHN METCALF.—Perhaps the career of no blind man in this country has been more remarkable than that of John Metcalf, or, as he was more commonly called, "Blind Jack," of Knaresborough. The following is a summary of his acquirements. He rode fearlessly alone, swam, and fished; was an excellent performer on the hautboy and other musical instruments; was a successful recruiting agent, and as a soldier was the life of the corps to which he belonged, in the bivouac or on the battle-field. He was a dealer in horses, fish, hay, wood, and woollen and other goods. He established public conveyances in towns, and between places which had not before enjoyed such advantages. He succeeded in building houses, and in making a great number of roads and bridges in the most satisfactory manner, in spite of strong competition from professional men, who enjoyed the advantages of perfect vision and long practical experience. Considered altogether, John Metcalf must ever stand out as an embodiment of strength of will, soundness of judgment, reckless disregard of danger, and extraordinary strength of physical constitution.

JOSEPH STRONG was blind from four years of age. At an early age he manifested great fondness for Music and the Mechanical Arts. Having constructed a violin, a harp, a flute, and a hautboy, he was ambitious to build an organ, and actually, when only 15 years old, completed one, much to the astonishment of those who examined it. He afterwards built another organ, upon which he played for the remainder of his life; and a third one which he constructed, was purchased by a gentleman in the Isle of Man. He also, with his own hands, constructed a weaver's loom; besides various articles of furniture, wearing apparel, &c.

THOMAS WILSON, the blind Turner and Bell-ringer of Dumfries, in Scotland, lost his sight in infancy. At 12 years of age, he became the chief bell-ringer of the Mid-Steeple of Dumfries. He early acquired the art of turning, which he practised with considerable success and profit. As a mechanic, he manifested extraordinary genius, having, among many other things, constructed, with his own hands, a lathe and a portable *break* for scutching lint.

THOMAS JAMES.—Perhaps, among the numerous blind of our own day, there are few more enterprising and self-dependant than Thomas James, of Ballarat, in Australia. Although an entire stranger to the country in which he lives (having emigrated from Cornwall, in England), it is wonderful how he makes his way, day after day, for a distance of seven miles or more, round about Ballarat. With only a dog as his companion, he seeks out and visits the blind, to instruct them in reading the " Old Old Story," to talk with them upon the things of the better land, and engage with them in prayer. This zealous labourer has already taught many of the sightless ones to read ; and among the number is a blind Chinese, whom he has not only taught to read, but to converse in English. " It is a touching sight " says one, in writing to a Ballarat newspaper, " to see this godly man setting forth on his labours of the day with his dog and stick, and his packet of books strapped to his back ; and it is remarkable how well he succeeds, having but one hand, and being an entire stranger to the country." For a long time, Thomas James laboured without the slightest remuneration ; but it is pleasing to know that his work has not been in vain. His efforts have gained for him many friends, and much gratitude from the blind. Government assistance has been solicited on his behalf ; and we hope, ere long, to hear that his labours have met with a due reward.

[A more detailed account of eminent blind persons will be given (D.V.) in a Biography of the Blind, which Dr. Moon is preparing for publication.]

EMBOSSED LITERATURE IN TYPE FOR THE BLIND

INVENTED BY W. MOON, LL.D.,

104, QUEEN'S ROAD, BRIGHTON.

ENGLISH LIST.

Bible.

Genesis 3 vols.
Exodus 2 "
Leviticus 2 "
Numbers 2 "
Deuteronomy 2 "
Joshua 2 "
Judges 2 "
1 Samuel 2 "
2 Samuel 2 "
1 Kings 2 "
2 Kings 2 "
1 Chronicles 2 "
2 Chronicles 2 "
Ezra to Esther, in 2 vols.
Job 2 vols.
Psalms 3 "
Proverbs 1 "
Ruth to Lamentations, in 1 vol.
Isaiah 3 vols.
Jeremiah 3 "
Ezekiel 3 "
Daniel 1 "
Hosea to Obadiah, in 1 vol.
Jonah to Malachi, in 2 vols.
Matthew 2 vols.
Mark 1 "
Luke 2 "
John 2 u
Acts 2 "
Romans to Corinthians, in 2 vols.
Galatians to Philemon, in 2 vols.
Hebrews to Jude, in 2 vols.
Revelation 1 "
The Minor Prophets and Epistles can be had separately.

For Beginners and the Aged.

Alphabet and Lord's Prayer (as a first lesson)
Spelling Lessons 1 and 2

FOR BEGINNERS *(continued)*.
Reading Lessons on Card, Nos. 1, 2, 3, 4, 5, 6,
" Nos. 1, 2, & 3, *(extra large type)*
Texts for the Aged and such as have very hard hands, parts 1, 2, 3, & 4, *(extra large type)*
First Lesson Book
John, Chapter 3
John " 14
John " 15
John " 16
John " 17
Life of Christ in Scripture words, in 3 vols
The above in 9 parts
Life of Christ, part 8 *(ex. lar. type)*
Life of Christ, part 9 *(ex. lar. type)*
The above are all printed in wide lines for Aged Persons and Learners.
Spelling Frames
Letters for ditto
Set of Wire Letters
Writing Frame, large
" " small
" Paper, with embossed lines.

Religious Works.

Pilgrim's Progress 2 vols.
Scotch Metrical Psalms 3 "
Scotch Paraphrases 1 "
Prayer-book Psalms 3 "
Morning and Evening Prayers and Litany 1 "
Epistles in Liturgy 2 "
Sinner's Friend 2 "
Morning Watches 3 "
Holy Communion 1 "
Collects 1 "
Telling Jesus
Lord's Supper (Prepar. Exercises)
Morning Portions (Bogatsky's)
Evening Portions (ditto)
Hele's Morning and Evening Prayers (selections from)

RELIGIOUS WORKS *(continued)*.

Texts of Consolation
Scripture Truths
Silent Comforter
Sunbeams for Human Hearts
The Glory of God
The Blood that Saveth
The Shorter Catechism
Uses of Difficulty
Thoughts of God—
  Infinite Condescension, &c., pt. 1
  Divine Challenge, &c.   " 2
  Tender Remonstrance, &c.   " 3
  Comfort for Bereaved, &c. " 4
The Lowest Place

Chapters and Psalms.

Sermon on the Mount
Matthew   chaps. 5
Matthew   u   6, 7
Luke   "   11
{ Luke   "   15
{ Ephesians "   2
Luke   "   18
John   "   1
John   "   3
John   "   6
John ·   "   10
John   "   14
John   "   15
John   u   16
John   "   17
John   "   18
Acts   "   9
1 Corinthians· " 15
2   "   "   5, 6
Hebrews   "   12
Proverbs   "   8
Psalms 34, 86, and 96
Psalms 40, 42 and 84
Psalms 32, 51, 130, and 143
Psalms 91, 139, and 147
Psalm 119
Isaiah   "   40
{ Isaiah   "   53
{ Psalms 23, 125
{ Isaiah   "   55
{ Psalms 27, 103
2 Kings   "   4
2 Kings   "   5

Poetry.

Bull's Hymns, 3 vols
Hymn of the Blind
Morning Hymns (by a Lady)
Evening Hymns (by a Lady)
Hymns on Resignation
Hymns on Hours of Sorrow

POETRY *(continued)*.

Hymns : Ashamed of Jesus
  "   All is known to Thee
  "   Precious Promises
  "   Need of Jesus
Sacred Poetry, Parts 1 and 2
Keble's Christian Year (selections from)
Revival Hymns, Parts 1 and 2
Children's Hymns
World in the Heart
Starless Crown
Christ our Example
Old Old Story
Herbert and Quarles (selections from)
Cotter's Saturday Night
Abide with Me, &c.
A Hymn, by J. Anderson, Esq.
Sankey's Hymns (selections from)
School Life

Educational Works.

History of England, vols. 1, 2, 3, 4
Geography, vols. 1, 2
Biblical Dictionary, vols. 1, 2, 3, 4
A Primer
First Spelling Book
Spelling Book, with meanings
Easy Reading Books (several)
Atlas of the Stars, &c.
Astronomy, vol. 1
Natural History, vol. 1
Grammar, part 1
Euclid, Book 1 (Diagrams)

Tales and Anecdotes.

Seaman's Leap for Life, &c.
Tiger Hunt, &c.
Falls of Niagara, &c.
Anecdotes of Dogs
Sagacity of a Lioness
Blind Beggar
Blind Irishman
Dying Robber
Luke Heywood
Time Enough Yet
Too Late
Sabbath Breaking
Soldier of Lucknow
Praying Willys
Highland Kitchen-maid
The Debt is Paid
Sam, the Converted Sailor
The Patchwork Quilt
Jesus met in Todmorden Vale
There is Room for You
Pious Teacher

TALES, &c. *(continued)*.

Lost Prayer Book
Eyes and Ears
Yeddie's First and Last Communion
Destruction of a Madrid Inquisition

REMARKABLE ANSWERS TO PRAYER.

Brave Emperor, &c.
Bristol Merchant, &c.
Negress and Her Nurse, &c.
Let him be Spared, &c.
Paying for Praying, &c.
Innkeeper's Family, &c.
Prayer Meeting Abandoned, &c.
Vessels Saved by Prayer, &c.
Learning to Pray, &c.
Two Praying Wives, &c.
Philip Henry's Promise, &c.
Irreverence Rebuked, &c.
Condemned Soldier, &c.
Loss of Family Prayer, &c.
Son's Admonition, &c.
King of Toobow, &c.
Prayer for a Lunatic Answered, &c.
Prayer for Fine Weather Answered, &c.
Guarded House, &c.
Beggar's Prayer, &c.
A Praying Mother, &c.
A Written Prayer Answered, &c.
Persecuting Father, &c.
Murderers Overawed, &c.

Memoirs.

Life of—
Capt. Cook
Zisca
G. Stephenson
R. Stephenson
Peter the Great
J. Vine Hall
James Watt
J. Metcalf
Christopher Columbus
Nicholas Bacon
Martin Luther
Sir William Herschell
Harriet Pollard
Eliza Cooter
Benjamin Franklin
Sir H. Davy
J. Ferguson, the Astronomer
Sir Isaac Newton
General Garibaldi
William Caxton

MEMOIRS *(continued)*.

Rev. A. Murray
Lady Jane Grey
William Carey
The Peel Family
Sir R. Arkwright
James Sharples
Josiah Wedgwood
Dr. Jenner
William Eade
Herbert Minton
Joseph Bramah
Henry Maudslay
Dr. Adam Clarke
Robert Bloomfield
Rev. W. Wedlock
Lord Nelson
John Davis
General Washington
Dr. Livingstone
Cranmer (Last Hours of)
Polycarp (Last Hours of)
Dr. Moon's Labours for the Blind (New Edition, vol. 1)
Early Years of H.R.H. the late Prince Consort
Queen's Journal, part 1, First Visit to Scotland
Queen's Journal, part 2, Visit to Blair Athole
Queen's Journal, part 3, West Tour
Queen's Journal, part 4, Life in the Highlands
The Prince and the Prayer
Gypson, Mrs. (Last Hours of), from a Diary

———o———

FOREIGN LIST.

DANISH.

John, chaps. 1 2, 3
John, chap. 14

NORSE.

John, chap. 14
John, " 1, 2, and 3

HINDUSTANEE.

Psalm 34
Matthew
John
John, chap. 3

BENGALI.

Luke, chap. 15

47

IRISH.

John, chap. 3
Acts " 9

ARMENIAN.

Psalms 34 and 86
John, chap. 3
Primer

GAELIC.

John
John, chap. 3
John 1, 2, and 3 (Epistles)
Psalms 34 and 86
Psalms 32, 51, 130, and 143

ITALIAN.

John, chap. 14
1 Peter
2 Peter

SPANISH.

John, chap. 3

JUDEO-SPANISH.

Psalm 51

NINGPO.

Matthew, chap. 2
Luke   ·

DUTCH.

Genesis
Luke
Acts
John
John, chap. 3
Psalm 34
Galatians
Ephesians
First Lesson Book

The Dutch portions are sold at the School for the Blind, Rotterdam.

GERMAN.

Genesis
Psalms
Psalms 34 and 86
Psalms 37 and 39
Psalms 90, 91, and 103
Psalms 125, 126, &c.
Matthew
John
John, chap. 3
John " 14

Mark
Birth of Christ
Galatians
Ephesians
Philippians
Colossians
John 1, 2, 3, Epistles
Luke
Old Old Story

WELSH.

John, chap. 14
John's 1st Epistle
John

FRENCH.

Psalms
Luke
John
John, chap. 3
John " 14
Acts
Romans
Revival Hymns, part
Attack of Wolves
Eliza Cooter

ARABIC.

Luke
John
John, chap. 3
John " 14
Sermon on the Mount
Galatians
Ephesians
Philippians
Colossians
Hebrews
James
1 Peter
2 Peter
1, 2, 3 John
Jude
Hymns
Grammar
Psalms 34, 86, and 96
Psalms 40 and 42

SWEDISH.

Psalms 34 and 86
Psalms 91 and 139
Zechariah
John
John, chap. 3
John " 14
Ephesians
Hymn Book, part 1

FOREIGN LIST *(continued).*

ARMENO-TURKISH.

Matthew
Matthew, chaps. 5, 6, 7

TAHITIAN.

John's Epistles, 1, 2, 3
John, chap. 3

SHANGHAI.

Sermon on the Mount

KAFFIR.

John, chap. 14
Hymn

PORTUGUESE.

John, chap. 3

GREEK (ANCIENT).

John, chap. 3

GREEK (MODERN).

John, chap. 3

RUSSIAN.

John, chap. 3

Maps.

SMALL EMBOSSED MAPS.

Canaan, Ancient Jerusalem, Italy, Russia, Plan of the Temple, Journeyings of the Israelites, Encampment, Plan of the Tabernacle, Golden Candlestick, Breastplate.

LARGE EMBOSSED MAPS,

WITH NAMES OF PLACES IN BLACK TYPE.

Palestine, England and Wales, Marching Order of the Israelites, Map illustrating Dr. Moon's Missionary Travels, St. Paul's Travels.

LARGE EMBOSSED MAPS,

WITHOUT ANY NAMES OF PLACES.

Europe, Africa, America, and Eastern Hemisphere.

Large Astronomical Maps and Diagrams.

Including, Maps of the Stars and the Milky Way, the Eclipses, Phases of the Moon, Comets, &c.

Many of the Works in this List have been Stereotyped at the expense of Benevolent Individuals as a kind of Legacy to the Blind : and any person who may wish to have a particular Chapter of the Bible, Hymn, or other worthy Work thus Stereotyped, can do so at the expense of 1/6 per page 8vo, and 2/6· per page 4to, in English, and 3/0 per page 4to in any Foreign Language ; a perfect copy of which will be presented to the Donor on the completion of the work ; but the plates will be retained as the property of the Charity.

Subscriptions, Banker's Drafts, Post-Office Orders, &c., towards the Embossing Fund, may be made payable to William Moon, LL.D., 104, Queen's Road, Brighton.

☞ It is particularly requested that care be taken that the full address, 104, *Queen's Road, Brighton,* be given to all letters addressed to Dr. William Moon, as occasionally letters have been delayed in transmission in consequence of an imperfect direction.

Edward Verrall, Printer, Brighton.

CPSIA information can be obtained
at www.ICGtesting.com
Printed in the USA
BVHW04*2125200918
527831BV00028B/981/P